ROBOTS AT PLAY

www.worldbook.com

Co-published by agreement between Shi Tu Hui and World Book, Inc.

Shi Tu Hui
Room 1807, Block 1,
#3 West Dawang Road
Chaoyang District, Beijing 100025
P.R. China

World Book, Inc.
180 North LaSalle Street
Suite 900
Chicago, Illinois 60601
USA

© 2026. All rights reserved. This volume may not be reproduced in whole or in part in any form without prior written permission from the publisher.

WORLD BOOK and the GLOBE DEVICE are registered trademarks or trademarks of World Book, Inc.

Library of Congress Control Number: 2025938165

Robots
ISBN: 978-0-7166-5814-6 (set, hard cover)

Robots at Play
ISBN: 978-0-7166-5820-7 (hard cover)

Also available as:
ISBN: 978-0-7166-5830-6 (soft cover)
ISBN: 978-0-7166-5840-5 (e-book)

WORLD BOOK STAFF

Writer: Jeff De La Rosa

Editorial

Vice President
Tom Evans

Senior Manager, New Content
Jeff De La Rosa

Associate Manager, New Content
William D. Adams

Content Creator
Elizabeth Huyck

Proofreader
Nathalie Strassheim

Graphics and Design

Senior Visual Communications Designer
Melanie Bender

Photo Editor
Rosalia Bledsoe

ACKNOWLEDGMENTS

Cover: © 35lab/Shutterstock; © Sony Corporation; © Petoi LLC; © Makeblock
4-5   © Tinnaporn Sathapornnanont, Shutterstock; © Sony Corporation
6-7   © Omer Faruk Boyaci, Shutterstock; Smithsonian Institution
8-9   Portrait of Jacques de Vaucanson (1784), oil on canvas by Joseph Boze; Academy of Sciences/Institut de France (Paris); Public Domain
10-11 © MediaNews Group/Orange County Register/Getty Images
12-13 © Cynthia Lee, Alamy Images; © Google DeepMind
14-15 © Jeremy Sutton-Hibbert, Alamy Images
16-17 © Rodrigo Reyes Marin/AFLO/Alamy Images
18-19 © RoboCup Federation
20-21 Peter Schulz (licensed under CC BY-SA 4.0); © RoboCup Federation
22-23 © SoftBank Robotics
24-25 © Francois Nel, Getty Images; © Philip Lange, Shutterstock
26-27 © Georgia Institute of Technolog; © dpa picture alliance/Alamy Images
28-29 © Georgia Institute of Technology
30-31 © Bettmann/Getty Images; © Jack Taylor, Getty Images
32-33 Public Domain; © CBS Toys
34-35 © Anki
36-37 © Hasbro; © Innvo Labs Corporation; © Petoi LLC
38-39 © Sony Corporation
40-41 © Good Moments/Shutterstock; © Ned Snowman, Shutterstock
42-43 © Ozobot & Evollve; © Sphero
44-45 © Makeblock; © Wonder Workshop, Inc; © Alesia Kan, Shutterstock
46-47 © IMAGO/Xinhua/Alamy Images; © dpa picture alliance/Alamy Images

Contents

- **4** Introduction
- **6** Automatons
- **10** Bringing Characters to Life
- **12** Let the Games Begin
- **14** ROBOT CHALLENGE: Get in the Game
- **16** Robot-sumo
- **18** The RoboCup
- **22** HELLO, MY NAME IS: Nao
- **24** Off to the Races
- **26** Robot Musicians
- **28** HELLO, MY NAME IS: Shimon
- **30** Toy Robots
- **34** HELLO, MY NAME IS: Vector
- **36** Robotic Pets
- **38** HELLO, MY NAME IS: AIBO
- **40** ROBOT RISK: Robot Relationships
- **42** Educational Robots
- **46** Hands-On Robotics
- **48** Glossary and Index

Terms defined in the glossary are in type **that looks like this** on their first appearance on any spread (two facing pages).

Introduction

Robots work in factories building cars, computers, and other things. Some robots toil around the home vacuuming carpets or mowing lawns. Many robots take on jobs that are dirty, dull, or dangerous. But where's the fun in that?

Some of the first mechanical robots were not built to do work. They were toys designed to entertain children and adults. These primitive playmates could do little more than roll around, beep, and light up. Over the years,

Retro robots
Robot-themed toys have been popular since the 1950's. Classic toy robots lacked true robotic abilities, but they inspired the imaginations of future inventors and engineers.

A modern toy robot can provide entertainment—and even companionship.

robots built for fun have grown up alongside their working cousins. Today's entertainment robot can be a powerful playmate, learning games, answering voice commands, and busting serious dance moves.

Robotic play is not just about having a good time. Teaching a robot to play soccer or a musical instrument, for example, involves some pretty complex challenges. In helping robots master these skills, inventors learn how to build better robots.

Automatons

Some of the first robotlike creations were made with amusement in mind. Long before there were robots, people marveled at devices called **automatons.** An automaton is a mechanical person or animal that mimics certain actions of the real thing. Automatons were often powered by steam, water, or wind-up springs.

Al-Jazari
This illustration shows the Muslim inventor al-Jazari working on a mechanical creation.

Yacht rock
Al-Jazari described a band of automaton musicians playing on a boat in his *The Book of Knowledge of Ingenious Mechanical Devices.*

Automatons are described in the myths, legends, and histories of many cultures. The Muslim inventor al-Jazari described several automatons in *The Book of Knowledge of Ingenious Mechanical Devices,* published in 1206. One of his designs was for a band of automaton musicians that played on a boat.

One incredible automaton has become known as the mechanical monk. It was probably built by a Spanish clockmaker during the 1500's and still works today. Wind the monk up, and it paces, moves its lips, and even kisses a cross, imitating a monk in prayer.

Duck daddy
Jacques de Vaucanson (above) made several famous automatons (below right), including one known as the Digesting Duck.

The French inventor Jacques de Vaucanson may be the most famous maker of **automatons** ever. In the 1700's, he built a mechanical flute player and another automaton that played tambourine. But his most famous automaton was the Digesting Duck. The duck could flap its wings, eat grain, and even go to the bathroom. The duck was not really digesting its food, though. It simply released fake waste from a secret compartment.

Also in the 1700's, the Swiss watchmaker Pierre Jaquet-Droz built three amazing automatons, called the Musician, the Draftsman, and the Writer. The Musician plays the organ.

The Draftsman draws pictures. The Writer dips a quill pen in ink and can write up to 40 letters. The motions were produced by a complex arrangement of gears inside.

Automatons thrilled the audiences of their day. But automatons lack something important in modern robots: **autonomy.** Autonomy is the ability of a machine to act—and react—without direct human control or help.

The Draftsman (drawer), the Musician, and the Writer are automatons of the 1700's that amazed audiences with their lifelike movements and seemingly artistic abilities.

Bringing Characters to Life

If you've ever been to a Disneyland or other theme parks, you might have met the modern descendants of Vaucanson's **automatons.** The moving mechanical pirates, presidents, and crocodiles that liven up many rides are also automatons, with gears and motors inside that produce the same action over and over.

But now that's changing. Real robots are starting to replace automatons in theme parks. They perform death-defying stunts, interact with visitors, and move around the parks alongside traditional human actors in costume.

Autonomous robots allow park designers to add characters that can't be performed by a human in a suit. These include very small characters, such as Yoda from Star Wars, and very large ones, such as dinosaurs. Disney is also making interactive robot versions of movie robot characters, if you yearn to shake hands with Wall-E or R2-D2.

Some older animatronics are also being updated with robotic components to make them more life-like and entertaining.

Acting the part

You might meet a real robot actor playing R2-D2 at some Disney theme parks. These entertainment robots are programmed to move around on their own and interact with visitors. It helps that R2-D2 does not need to speak.

Let the Games Begin

If you like to play sports, modern robots might help you get an edge. Many sports teams now use high-tech cameras and computers to analyze play and help players improve their form. The latest robotic pitching machines for baseball practice don't just lob out balls. They can mimic the styles of different pitchers and adjust in real time as a player practices.

Table tennis, also known as ping-pong, is a fairly simple game—just two paddles, a net, and a ball. But it challenges humans and robots alike with its lightning-fast play. Robot makers have

Forpheus is a ping-pong-playing robot that looks a bit like a mechanical spider. It can help train human players by projecting onto the table where its shot is going to go.

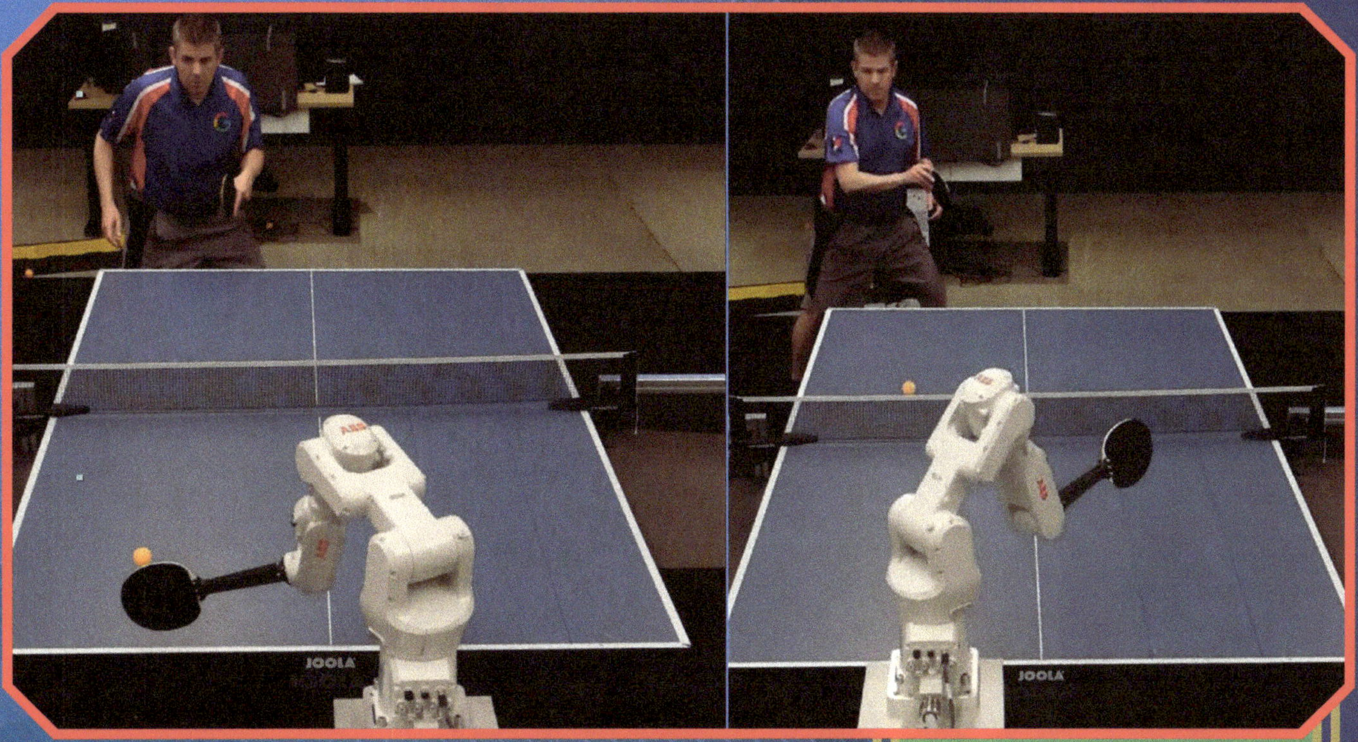

designed several ping-pong-playing 'bots, trying out different body styles. The Forpheus robot from Japan stands over the table on a tripod, looking a bit like a giant mechanical spider. The robot uses visual **sensors** to track the ball and its human opponent. A robotic arm hangs down from the spider's body, swinging the paddle into position.

In 2024, engineers at Google's DeepMind project unveiled their new ping-pong 'bot. The 'bot itself is a ordinary industrial mechanical arm, aided by overhead cameras. The arm's motion is powered by sophisticated **machine learning** that allow the 'bot to quickly react to shots and plan its own in real time.

Ping-Pong bot
Google's DeepMind ping-pong computer, fitted with a standard robotic arm, beat most human beginners but not expert players.

[13]

Robots themselves don't enjoy playing sports (or anything else, because they have no emotions). So why build sports-playing robots? The answer is that sports provide a challenge for robot makers. In building robots that are good at sports, engineers learn to build robots that are better at many other tasks. Sports are a particularly good challenge because they are both difficult and simple.

Sports are difficult because they require the ability to act—and react—quickly. Imagine a robot trying to play catch. The robot must first sense the ball—not only where it is, but how it is moving. Then, the robot must move to catch the ball, all in the blink of an eye. Team sports, such as soccer, present a much greater challenge. They require multiple robots to work together.

In other ways, sports are simple. Sports have rules, and the computer "brains" of robots are good at handling rules. Even an advanced AI robot might have trouble predicting all that could happen on a busy city sidewalk. On a soccer field, a robot faces a much more limited set of challenges.

> **"I'll be back…for the next match."**
> Humans have the upper hand for now, but robotic athletes could one day play to win.

Robot-sumo

Robot fighting competitions, or battles, have thrilled fans since the late 1990's. In these contests, robots attempt to disable opposing robots or push them out of a ring. Often the robots are fitted with hammers, saws, and other weapons. In early contests, most of the 'bots were remote-controlled, with little or no **autonomy.** But now more are fighting on their own.

Robot-sumo is a competition inspired by traditional Japanese sumo wrestling. As in human sumo, two competitors face off inside a ring. The goal is to push one's opponent out. Robot-sumo is fought by boxy, wheeled, fully **autonomous** robots. The robots use wedge-shaped scoops to lift their opponents and push them out of the ring.

The simplest robot-sumo fighters zip heedlessly around the ring, hoping to catch their opponents off guard. Others use complicated **sensors,** monitoring their opponent's movement in an effort to gain an advantage.

Robot-sumo competitors win by pushing their opponent out of the ring, much like human sumo wrestlers.

The RoboCup

Perhaps the most famous robot sports competition is the Robot World Cup, also called the RoboCup. RoboCup is an international soccer tournament for robots that began in 1997. The robots score the goals, but the real contest is between teams of robot designers and programmers, who compete to field robots that can outmove, outkick, and outscore the competition.

Dribbling Daleks
These wheeled robots work together to exterminate the opposition—on the soccer field, of course.

The RoboCup has several different size leagues, from miniature swarm-bots to human-sized robots that play with a normal soccer ball. There are also leagues for small and large **humanoid** robots. Team sizes range from 2 to 11 players.

The RoboCup is a fun time for all. But its organizers also have a serious goal of improving robots' ability to move around and act together. By 2050 they hope to field a team of robots capable of beating human World Cup champions.

Pelébots?
Humanoid robot soccer players move much more slowly than robots on wheels. How do humans manage to run without falling over?

The wheeled robots usually play the best soccer. But it is the **humanoid** matches that draw the most fans. There are three humanoid divisions, two for free-form robots, and one in which all contestants use the same robot, the 23-inch- (58-cm-) tall Nao.

In the free-form divisions, the challenge is to build robots that walk, kick, and turn without falling over. Falling over is common. In the Nao division, teams compete using identical, pre-built robots. This allows them to focus on programming the robots, rather than building them. This

A small Nao humanoid robot kicks the ball while its goalkeeper teammate looks on.

A RoboCup match featuring humanoid players attracts a large crowd of spectators, though not quite as raucous as the fans at a professional soccer match.

league first fielded teams of a robotic dog named AIBO. In 2008, it began using the humanoid robot Nao. The company that produced Nao is no longer making them, but there are plenty of old ones around for robot soccer enthusiasts.

Soccer is a surprisingly complex game. Players have to be aware of the constantly changing situation on the field. And, they have to work together to score against opponents—just like real soccer teams.

HELLO, MY NAME IS:

Nao

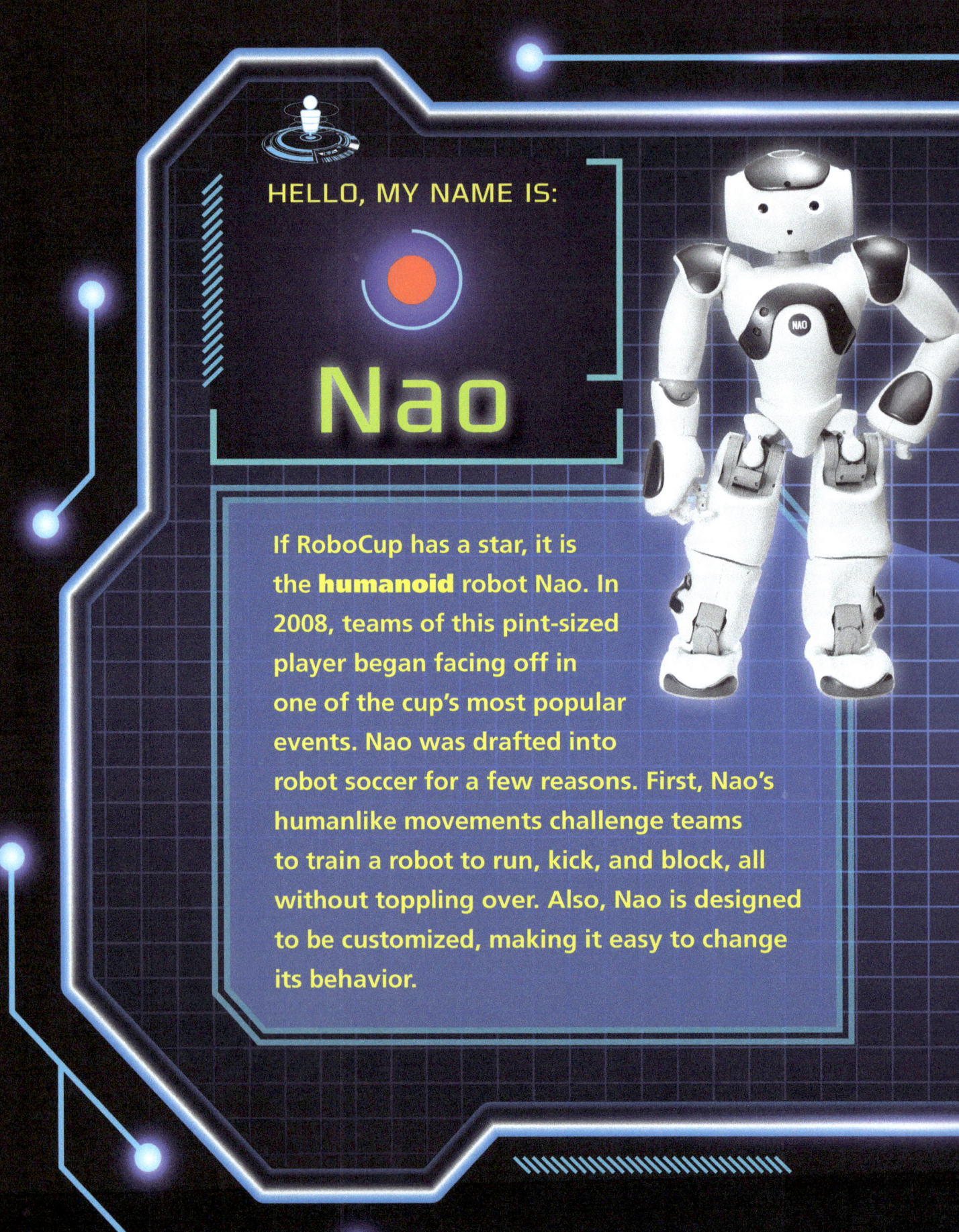

If RoboCup has a star, it is the **humanoid** robot Nao. In 2008, teams of this pint-sized player began facing off in one of the cup's most popular events. Nao was drafted into robot soccer for a few reasons. First, Nao's humanlike movements challenge teams to train a robot to run, kick, and block, all without toppling over. Also, Nao is designed to be customized, making it easy to change its behavior.

AUTONOMY

HIGH

Nao generally performs tasks on its own, but it can also be operated via remote control.

HEAD'S UP!

Nao speaks and listens, using four directional microphones to locate sounds. It sees with two high-definition cameras and can learn to recognize shapes and faces.

Staying upright is a major challenge for humanoid robots. Nao uses a **sensor** package to help prevent falls.

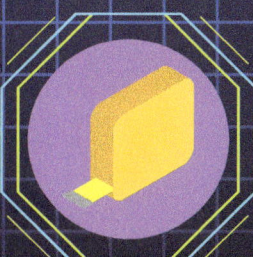

HEIGHT

23 inches (58 centimeters)

MORE THAN JUST A JOCK

Schools and laboratories have used Nao to test out all sorts of robot ideas. Nao has even been tried as a **therapy robot,** working with children with educational difficulties.

MAKER

Nao is made by Aldebaran Robotics of Paris, France.

Off to the Races

Robotic technology has changed a surprising sport—camel racing. Camel racing is a popular pastime in parts of the Middle East. Traditionally, the camels have been ridden by children, because camels carrying less weight go faster. But races are dangerous, and child jockeys are often abused and mistreated. These problems have led inventors to develop robot jockeys. Robot jockeys rode their first official camel race in 2005, in the nation of Qatar.

Giddy-up! Remote-controlled "robot" jockeys drive the competitors in this camel race.

Snappy dressers
Robot jockeys can be decked out in riding silks like their human counterparts. Many even have cute little riding caps.

The robot jockey is a lightweight device that sits on the camel's back. Its hinged arms hold a whip and the reins. Most models also have a speaker for giving voice commands. The jockeys are not true robots in the traditional sense. They have no **autonomy**—the ability to act without human control. Rather, the jockeys are operated by remote control from vehicles that follow alongside the thundering camels.

Robot jockeys are not true robots. But their success raises the possibility that robots could one day replace human athletes in other punishing pastimes, such as boxing or football.

Robot Musicians

Sports are fun for some, but others prefer more creative pursuits. Over the years, engineers have built many robots that can play music. These machines are not just mindless **automatons** like Jacques de Vaucanson's flute player. Some of them can write their own songs and even jam with human musicians.

In 1992, inventors at the Autonomous University of Puebla, Mexico, introduced a piano-playing robot named Don Cuco El Guapo. El Guapo means *the handsome*. But the name was probably meant as a joke. With his clear plastic body and mechanical insides, Don Cuco is not much of a looker. But, this **humanoid** pianist sure can play. Don Cuco has cameras for eyes and can play keyboard from sheet music.

The robot drummer Haile (pronounced *HY lee*) can do something many robots cannot—it can *improvise* (make up music as it plays). Haile is a mostly wooden robot designed to play along with a human drummer. The robot detects sound through a microphone and plays along, adjusting to changes in rhythm, tempo, and volume. Haile was built in 2006 by researchers at the Georgia Institute of Technology in Atlanta.

Jam session
The robot drummer Haile can drum along with human players and even make up new music as it goes.

Metal metal
What could be more metal than a Metal band made of metal? Compressorhead is an all-robot band that plays heavy metal music on real instruments from midi (computer music) files. They even dance.

HELLO, MY NAME IS: Shimon

When it comes to playing music, humans have a lot of advantages over robots. But the robot musician Shimon has something that human players do not—four arms. Shimon uses them to play a xylophonelike instrument called the marimba. A foursome of flippers is not the only trick up Shimon's sleeve. The robot can actually compose songs using **artificial intelligence** techniques. Shimon's computer "brain" studies thousands of pop, classical, jazz, and other songs. Shimon searches for common patterns among songs, using this information to strike out original tunes.

AUTONOMY
HIGH

Shimon can write its own songs, but it needs a few notes of inspiration from a human.

PLAYING IN THE BAND

Shimon can also improvise, jamming along with human musicians.

REPERTOIRE

Shimon knows more than 5,000 whole songs and 2 million other musical figures.

MAKER

Researchers at the Georgia Institute of Technology in Atlanta created Shimon.

STYLE

Shimon's compositions have been described as a cross between jazz and classical.

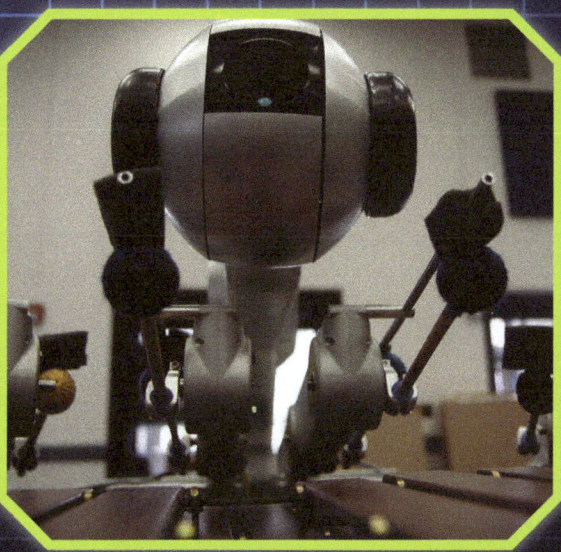

Toy Robots

High-tech robot musicians are impressive, but don't exactly fit in the toy box. Luckily, there are lots of playful robots that do.

Toy robots first became popular during the 1950's. Robert the Robot thrilled many kids of this era. The boxy plastic robot stood 14 inches (36 centimeters) tall and wheeled around by remote control. Robert's abilities were modest by modern standards. He could play a few recorded words, light up his eyes, and hold onto small objects placed in his robot grip.

The robot toys of the 1950's were not exactly robots in the modern sense—they had no **sensors** or **autonomy.** But they did inspire an interest in robotics in a generation of children.

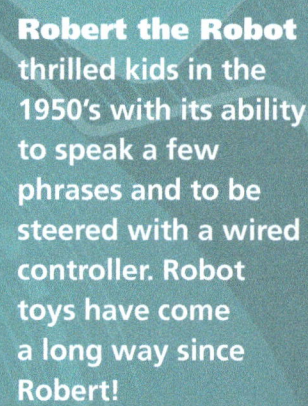

Robert the Robot thrilled kids in the 1950's with its ability to speak a few phrases and to be steered with a wired controller. Robot toys have come a long way since Robert!

[30]

The next toy robot craze happened during the 1980's. It was probably sparked in large part by the movie *Star Wars* (1977) and its sequels. Those movies featured a number of mechanical "droids," including the lovable pals C-3PO and R2-D2. *Droid* is short for **android,** a kind of advanced **humanoid** robot.

Unlike C-3PO and R2-D2, toy robots of the 1980's still did not have much **autonomy.** But they did feature some fairly advanced electronics. The toy

The lovable R2-D2 and other droids in the "Star Wars" movies renewed interest in toy robots in the 1970's and 1980's.

More like Maxx Plastic?
Maxx Steele was the hottest toy robot of the 1980's. It had only a few simple abilities, but it was a big step up from Robert the Robot.

robot Maxx Steele, for example, could grab and carry small items, play simple computer games, and even beep out a few tunes.

In the early 2000's, advances in technology led to better and better toy robots. Fairly affordable toy robots could finally balance, sense their surroundings, and be controlled with phone **apps**.

HELLO, MY NAME IS:

Vector

Looking for a pint-sized playmate? Meet Vector, one of a growing number of tiny toy robots powered by AI. Vector looks a little like a miniature bulldozer or forklift. But he is not a heavy lifter. Instead, he uses his forklift-like arm to play games, by pushing, stacking, and flipping special blocks. With his animated eyes and lively chirps, Vector is designed to mimic human feelings, including happiness and frustration. If Vector loses a game, he might throw a miniature tantrum, furrowing his brow and shaking his arm. If he wins, Vector might celebrate with a victory dance.

AUTONOMY

HIGH

Vector is not a passive plaything. If he gets bored, he may start to explore his surroundings or challenge you to a game.

LITTLE HELPER

Vector can wake you up, take photos, report the news and weather, chat, and find information on the internet.

CARTOON CUTIE

Vector's reactions were created with the help of Carlos Baena, an animator who worked on the robot film *WALL-E* (2008).

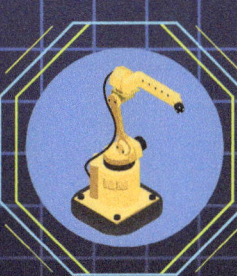

MAKER

Vector is made by the American robotics company Digital Dream Labs.

Robotic Pets

Would you rather have a dog or a robot? How about a pet that is both?

The Tiger Electronics company started a robotic pet craze in 1998 with the release of the robotic toy Furby. Furby looked a little like a fuzzy cartoon owl. It could move its eyes, mouth, and ears. Furby was a noisy toy. It had a habit of babbling in a made-up language called

Furby robotic toys have delighted children and annoyed parents since 1998. A new model was released in 2023.

Furbish. Over time, the robot used more and more English words. Furby's learning ability turned out to be exaggerated. But millions of the toys were sold, showing that people were interested in robot pets.

A wide range of robot pets became available during the 2000's. Robot dogs led the way, with popular models such as AIBO (pronounced *EYE bow)*, Tekno, and Poo-Chi. But there were also robot cats, birds, dinosaurs, and other animals. Robot pets range from fairly simple toys to advanced models that mimic real pet behaviors.

Pocket dog
Bittle (left) is a small robot dog that can be programmed by its owner.

Back from extinction
The baby dinosaur robot Pleo (right) had advanced sensors and moved realistically, but it was very expensive for a toy.

[37]

HELLO, MY NAME IS:

AIBO

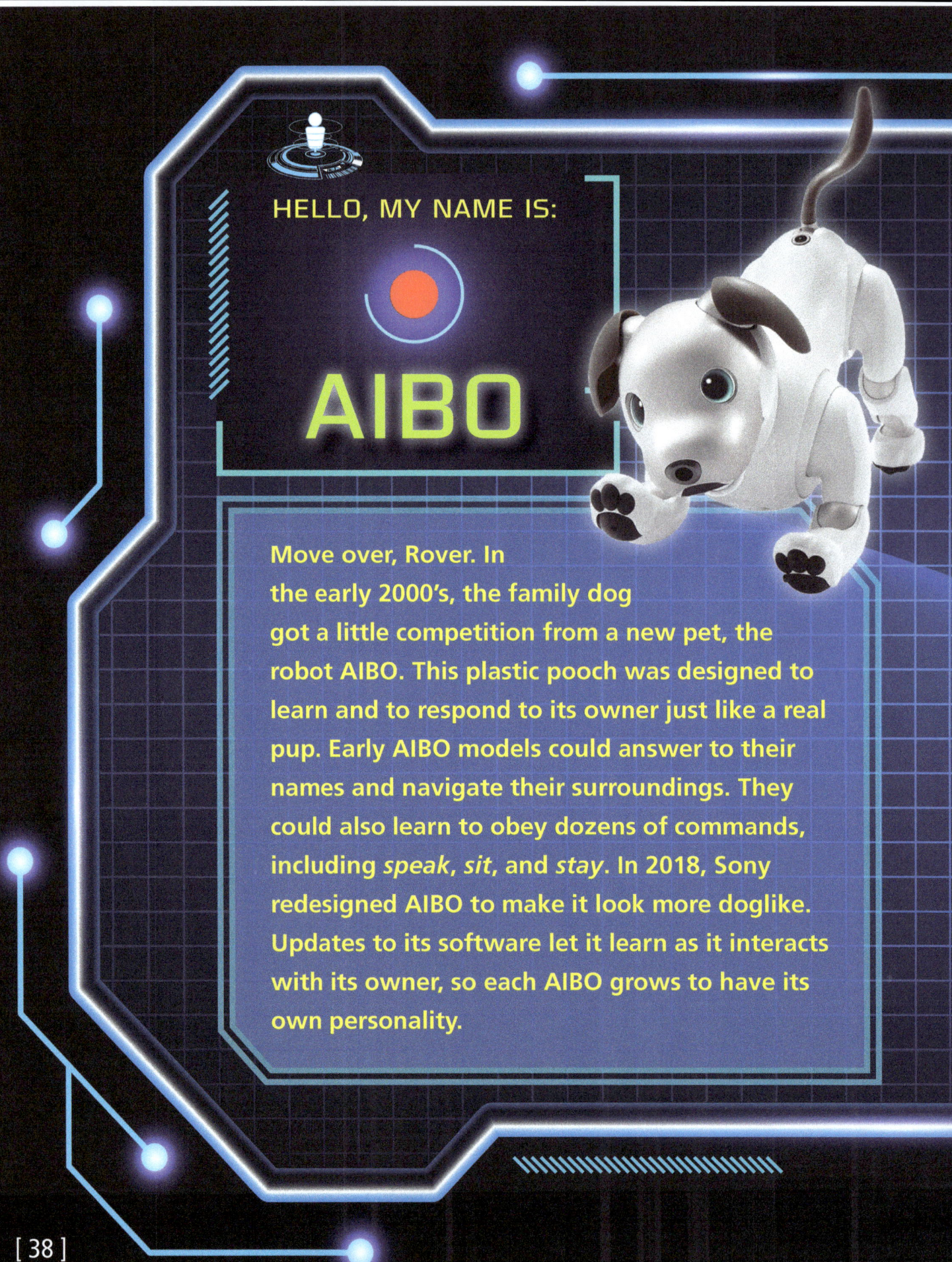

Move over, Rover. In the early 2000's, the family dog got a little competition from a new pet, the robot AIBO. This plastic pooch was designed to learn and to respond to its owner just like a real pup. Early AIBO models could answer to their names and navigate their surroundings. They could also learn to obey dozens of commands, including *speak*, *sit*, and *stay*. In 2018, Sony redesigned AIBO to make it look more doglike. Updates to its software let it learn as it interacts with its owner, so each AIBO grows to have its own personality.

AUTONOMY

HIGH

AIBO can do many things that a real-life dog can do.

SOCCER STAR

Teams of AIBO robots competed in the Four-Legged League of the Robot World Cup from 1999 to 2008.

WHAT'S IN A NAME?

AIBO is short for *A*rtificial *I*ntelligence *BO*t. The word *aibo* means *companion* in Japanese.

SO REAL

AIBO is programmed to ignore commands now and then, just like a real dog. It also "eats" digital food.

ROBOT RESURRECTION

Sony discontinued AIBO in 2008, but brought it back in 2018 with an updated design and advanced features.

MAKER

AIBO is manufactured by the Japanese tech company Sony.

The original AIBO had a more mechanical look.

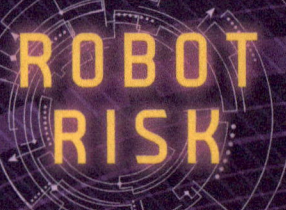

ROBOT RISK

Robot Relationships

Toy and pet robots can be fun playmates. But some experts worry that it is too easy for robots to trick humans emotionally. A robot cat, for example, can be programmed to rub up against people and purr. This does not mean that the robot actually likes the person, or feels anything at all.

Interacting with robots is different from the complex emotional bond that can be shared between living things. Studies have shown that animals develop

"Who's a good boy?" It can be difficult for children to distinguish important differences between robots and living things. Adults can help through clear communication.

Digital devotion Children and adults can develop a strong emotional attachment to such 'bots as the robot dog AIBO. In 2018, a Buddhist temple in Japan hosted a funeral service for more than 100 out-of-service AIBO's set to be scrapped for spare parts.

deep emotional responses to people they are bonded with. Robots can only fake this kind of connection. Is that a problem?

Studies have shown that children age 3 to 4 are not sure how much robots know. Children age 6 to 10 may believe robots are smarter than themselves, even though this is generally not true. This confusion can make it especially easy for robots to play on children's emotions.

Other experts think it is okay for children to explore an emotional connection with a robot. They consider it similar to having an imaginary friend, a common part of childhood. Adults can help by communicating clearly about the capabilities and limitations of robots.

[41]

Educational Robots

Many robot engineers start out by playing with robot toys, programming them to do interesting things. Playing with robots can help people learn about technology, develop problem-solving skills, and collaborate. In fact, many robots are designed with education in mind.

Directing robots is a super fun way to learn simple computer programming skills, also called coding. Users create

Drawn along
In one of its modes, the robot Evo follows lines drawn by marker. Evo may perform a simple action, such as turning around or spinning in place, upon passing a particular sequence of colors.

a set of instructions for the robot, often using an **app.** The robot then follows the instructions. This is a great way to learn coding language and how to set up commands to get the desired action.

Two simple programmable robots are Bolt and Evo. The Bolt looks like a little plastic ball. Evo is more like a dome that scurries along on little wheels. Both robots can be programmed to roll, turn, and light up using a smartphone or tablet.

The Sphero Bolt can be controlled remotely using a smartphone **app,** but users can also create programs for the robot to follow.

There are many kits that provide all the parts to let kids both build and program their own robots. Some use block-based programming languages. Others use common languages like Python.

One of the most popular educational robotics programs is LEGO Spike. LEGO's first robot kits, Mindstorms, got many kids into building robots. LEGO robotics combine traditional LEGO blocks with robotic motors and **sensors,** powered by a programmable "smart brick." This makes it easy and fun to build a robot imagined entirely by you. Several robot competitions, including FIRST Robotics, have special divisions for LEGO robots.

Robots can also help kids learn in other ways. Some interactive robots are programmed with **artificial**

Build your dream 'bot with a handy kit. Makeblock is just one of many robot-building kits that provide everything you need to start building and programming your very own robot.

Brick 'bots
LEGO Spike kits enable children, teens, and adults to build and program all kinds of robots using LEGO bricks and simple block programming.

intelligence (AI) that allows them to chat with kids, tell stories, or sing songs. Robots can also be tasked to help with math or language drills or to offer encouragement when its time to practice piano.

[45]

Hands-On Robotics

Want to get started making robots? Jump right in!

RoboCup Junior

RoboCup Soccer is large international robotics competition in which teams of robots of various sizes face off to play soccer. RoboCup also hosts contests for rescue and industrial robots. Younger robot builders can get started with RoboCup Junior League.

The RoboCup Junior League has several divisions for different kinds of robot-building challenges. Robots are built and programmed entirely by teams of kids.

Soccer: Fully autonomous small robots play a short soccer game either one-on-one or two-on-two against robots from an opposing team.

Rescue: Autonomous robots compete to complete a rescue challenge, following paths, negotiating rough ground, and locating "victims" within a disaster area.

RoboCup ready
Young challengers get ready to face off in an open-form soccer match at RoboCup Junior in Hefei, China, in 2015. RoboCup international finals are held in a different country each year.

OnStage: For the more artistically inclined, the OnStage league asks contestants to present a dramatic or artistic piece that involves humans and robots working together, in costume.

Time to get your game on!

Also check out:
• FIRST Robotics LEGO League
• Scratch (MIT Media Lab)
• National Robotics Challenge

Or ask at your local school, library, or maker space.

Glossary

actuator a device, such as a motor, that provides movement to a robot.

android a type of humanoid robot designed to look as humanlike as possible.

artificial intelligence (AI) the ability of a computer system to process information in a manner similar to human thought or to exhibit humanlike behavior.

automation the use of machines to perform tasks that require decision making.

autonomy the degree to which a robot can make decisions without input from a human operator to achieve a goal.

collaborative robot (cobot) an industrial robot designed to work closely with people and share workspaces with them.

effector the part of the robot's body, such as a wheel or a gripper, that is moved by an actuator and interacts with the environment to perform an action.

hardware the physical parts of a computer.

humanoid shaped like or resembling a human.

industrial robot a robot that works in a factory to help create a product.

machine learning a field of artificial intelligence that involves computer programs learning from examples and from experience.

sensor a device that takes in information from the outside world and translates it into code.

software a general term for computer programs. A computer program is mostly made up of a sequence of instructions. The instructions tell a computer what to do and how to do it.

structured environment in robotics, an area in which a robot operates that has been specially designed to reduce the number of unexpected occurrences while the robot is working. The flow of people, vehicles, and items not involved in the robot's task is usually restricted.

unstructured environment in robotics, an area in which a robot operates that has not been specially designed for it. People, vehicles, and other things may pass through the area in which the robot works.

Index

A
AIBO (robot), 21, 37-39, 41
al-Jazari, 6-7
androids, 32
apps, 33, 43
artificial intelligence (AI), 28, 34, 44-45
automatons, 6-9, 10, 26
autonomy, 9

B
Bittle (toy), 37
Bolt (robot), 43
Book of Knowledge of Ingenious Mechanical Devices, The, 7

C
camel racing, 24-25
coding, 42-43
Compressorhead (band), 27

D
DeepMind, 13
Digesting Duck, 8
Disneyland, 10-11
Don Cuco El Guapo (robot), 26
Draftsman (automaton), 8-9
droids, 32
drummer, 26-27

E
educational robots, 42-45
Evo (robot), 42, 43

F
FIRST Robotics, 44, 47
Forpheus (robot), 12-13
Furby (toy), 36-37

G
Google, 13

H
Haile (robot), 26-27
humanoids, 15, 20-23, 26, 32

J
Jaquet-Droz, Pierre, 8-9
jockeys, robot, 24-25

L
LEGO: Mindstorms, 44; Spike, 44-45

M
machine learning, 13
Makeblock, 45
marimba, 28
Maxx Steele (toy), 32-33
mechanical monk, 7
music, 5, 7-9, 26-29
Musician (automaton), 8-9

N
Nao (robot), 20-23

P
pets, robotic, 36-41
ping pong. *See* table tennis
Pleo (toy), 37
programming, 42-43

R
R2-D2 (movie robot), 10-11, 32
rescue (competition), 46
Robert the Robot, 30-31, 33
RoboCup, 18-21, 39, 46-47
Robot-sumo, 16-17
robots, 4-5; early, 6-9; educational, 42-45; musical, 5, 7-9, 26-29; pet, 36-41; sports, 12-25; toy, 4-5, 30-35

S
sensors, 15, 16, 23, 44, 45
Shimon (robot), 28-29
soccer, 5, 13, 18-22, 39, 46
Sony, 38-39
Sphero (company), 43
sports, 12-25
Star Wars (movie), 32

T
table tennis, 12-13
technology, 33, 42, 44
therapy robots, 23
Tiger Electronics, 36
toy robots, 4-5, 30-35

V
Vaucanson, Jacques de, 8, 27
Vector (robot), 34-35

W
World Cup (soccer), 19
Writer (automaton), 8-9

www.ingramcontent.com/pod-product-compliance
Lightning Source LLC
Chambersburg PA
CBHW061254170426
43191CB00041B/2423